# Subtracting Spiders

By Nick Rebman

**www.littlebluehousebooks.com**

Little Blue House is distributed by North Star Editions:
sales@northstareditions.com | 888-417-0195

Produced for Little Blue House by Red Line Editorial.

Photographs ©: iStockphoto, cover; Shutterstock Images, 4 (spiders), 4 (wood), 7 (spiders), 7 (book), 9 (spiders), 9 (floor), 11 (spiders), 11 (grass), 13 (spiders), 13 (sand), 15 (spiders), 15 (dirt), 16 (top left), 16 (top right), 16 (bottom left), 16 (bottom right)

**Library of Congress Control Number: 2020900840**

**ISBN**
978-1-64619-171-0 (hardcover)
978-1-64619-205-2 (paperback)
978-1-64619-273-1 (ebook pdf)
978-1-64619-239-7 (hosted ebook)

Printed in the United States of America
Mankato, MN
012021

## About the Author

Nick Rebman enjoys reading, walking his dog, and traveling to places where he doesn't speak the language. He lives in Minnesota.

# Table of Contents

# Subtracting Spiders

I had three spiders on the table.

My friend took two spiders.

Now I have one spider.

I had four spiders on the book.

My friend took one spider.

Now I have three spiders.

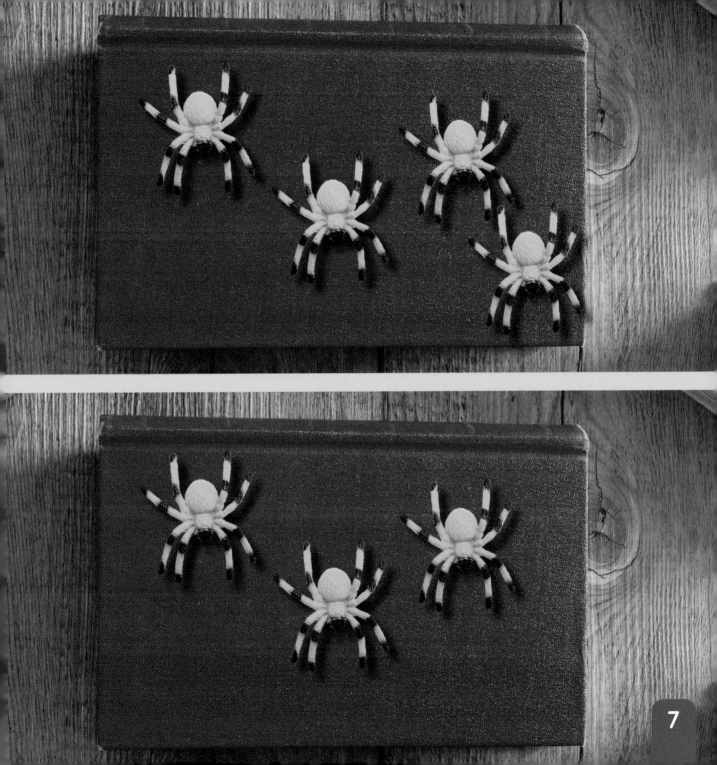

I had six spiders on the floor.

My friend took one spider.

Now I have five spiders.

I had seven spiders on the grass.

My friend took six spiders.

Now I have one spider.

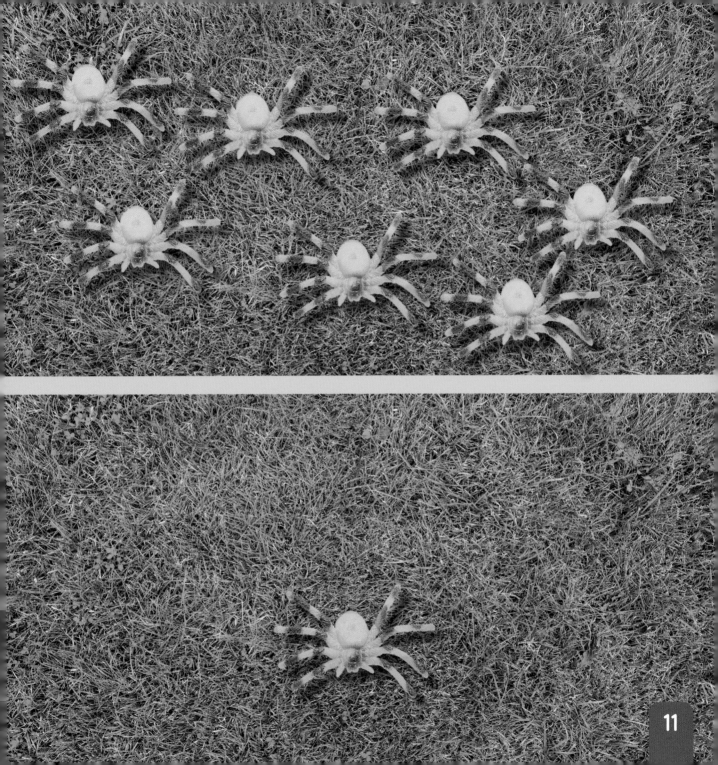

I had eight spiders on the sand.

My friend took six spiders.

Now I have two spiders.

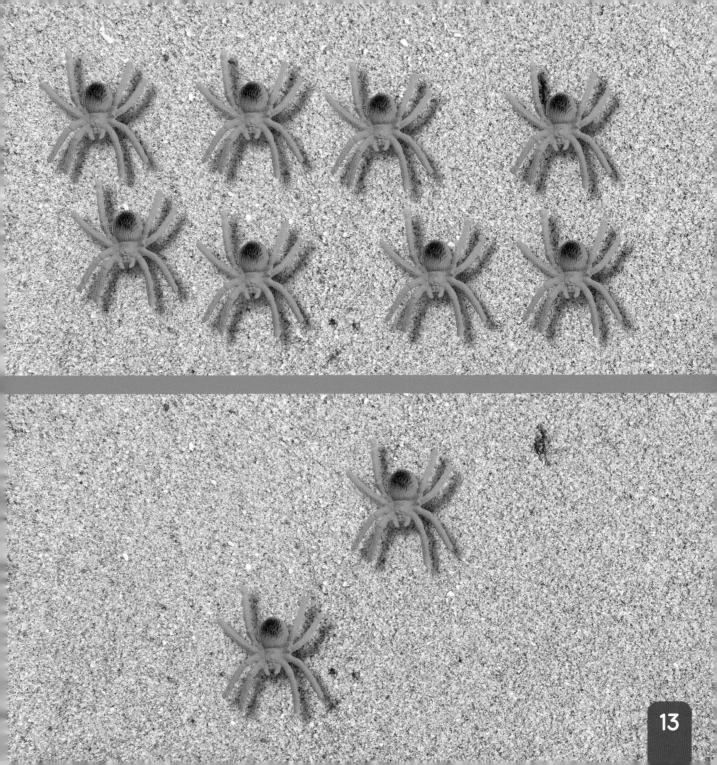

I had nine spiders on the dirt.

My friend took six spiders.

Now I have three spiders.

# Glossary

**dirt**

**spider**

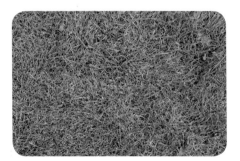

**grass**

**table**

# Index